SHAKESPEARE'S WILL

AMS PRESS
NEW YORK

SHAKESPEARE'S WILL,

COPIED FROM THE

ORIGINAL IN THE PREROGATIVE COURT,

Preserving the Interlineations,

AND

FACSIMILES

OF

THE THREE AUTOGRAPHS OF THE POET.

With a few Preliminary Observations,

BY

J. O. HALLIWELL, ESQ., F.R.S., F.S.A.

LONDON:
JOHN RUSSELL SMITH,
4, OLD COMPTON STREET, SOHO SQUARE.
1851.

Library of Congress Cataloging in Publication Data

Shakespeare, William, 1564-1616.
   Shakespeare's will.

   1. Shakespeare, William, 1564-1616 — Will.
  2. Shakespeare, William, 1564-1616 — Autographs.
I. Title.
PR2908.H3   1974   822.3'3   79-144631
ISBN 0-404-03086-6

Reprinted from an original in the Folger Shakespeare Library
Folger Call Number: PR
                    2908
                    S72

Reprinted from the edition of 1851, London
First AMS edition published, 1974
Manufactured in the United States of America

AMS Press, Inc.
New York, N.Y. 10003

PREFACE.

SOME years ago, an attempt was made to present Shakespeare's Will in a form which should clearly exhibit its original character, with the interlineations and corrections, to those who had not seen that most interesting document. The authorities of the Prerogative Court stedfastly refused to allow a facsimile of the Will to be made, and the only course which remained was to print it as nearly in its original form as was practicable with modern type. This was executed in the three following leaves (representing the three sheets of common legal brief paper, on which the original is written), by the late MR. T. RODD, who, however, having discovered some errors in the transcription, carefully suppressed them from the public.

On a minute examination of MR. RODD's copy, it was discovered that the chief errors of importance had been made in the preliminary sentence, and that, on the whole, it was a tolerably accurate transcript of the Will. Thus, at the commencement, *unice* should be *nunc ;* *Rx* should be the letter *R.* with a contraction, of course standing for *regis ;* *Sextie* should be *Scotie ;* and *January, Januarii.* In the Latin at the end, we have *Magistri Willielmi* for *Magistro Willielmo,* etc. On p. 1, l. 27, we should have, *are to paie her.* Lower down, *attaine* should be *att anie,* the word *time* having been accidentally omitted in the original. At p. 2, l. 7, the word *her* is cancelled in the manuscript.

It will be observed, that although these are, for the most part, very careless oversights, they do not prevent the reader having a much clearer view of the character of the original, than in any edition of the Will that has yet been published; and it was thought that an acceptable service would be rendered to the Shakespearian student by its publication. The impression is limited to *one hundred* copies.

AVENUE LODGE, BRIXTON HILL.
May 1851.

[SHAKSPEARE'S WILL.]

Vicesimo Quinto Die ~~January~~ ^Mtij^ Anno Regni Dñi nri Jacobi ~~unice~~ ^nunc^ Rx̸ Anglie
&c. Decimo quarto & ~~Sextie~~ xlix° Annoq, Dñi 1616

T. W^{mj} Shackspeare

In the name of god Amen I Willim̃ Shackspeare of Stratford vpon Avon in the countie of warr gent in ṗfect health & memorie god be praysed doe make & Ordayne this my last will & testam^t in mañ & forme followeing That ys to saye ffirst I Comend my Soulē into the hands of god my Creator hoping & assuredlie beleeving through th onelie meritts of Jesus Christe my Saviour to be made ptaker of lyfe everlastinge And my bodye to the Earth whereof yt ys made Itm̃ I Gyve & bequeath vnto my ~~sonne &~~ Daughter Judyth One hundred & ffyftie pounds of lawful English money to be paied vnto her in mañ & forme followeing That ys to saye One hundred pounds ^in discharge of her marriage porcõn^ wthin one yeare after my deceas wth consideracõn after the Rate of twoe Shillings in the pound for soe long tyme as the same shalbe vnpaied vnto her after my Deceas & the ffyftie pounds Residewe thereof vpon her Surrendring ^of^ or gyving of such sufficient securitie as the overseers of this my Will shall like of to Surrender or grañte All her estate and Right that shall discend or come vnto her after my deceas or ^that shee^ nowe hath of in or to one Copiehold teñte wth thapṗtennc̃s lyeing and being in Stratford vpon Avon aforesaied in the saied countie of warr being pcell or holden of the manno^r of Rowington vnto my Daughter Susanna Hall & her heires for ever Itm̃ I Gyve & bequeath vnto my saied Daughter Judith One hundred & ffyftie pounds more if she or Anie issue of her bodie be Lyvinge att thend of three yeares next ensueing the Daie of the Date of this my Will during wch tyme my executo^{rs} ^are^ to paie her consideracõn from my deceas according to the Rate aforesaied And if she Dye wthout issue of her bodye then my Will ys & I Doe gyve & bequeath One Hundred Pounds thereof to my neece Elizabeth Hall & the ffiftie Pounds to be sett fourth by my executo^{rs} during the lief of my Sister Johane Harte & the vse & ṗffitt thereof cominge shalbe payed to my saied Sister Ione & after her deceas the saied l^{li} shall Remaine Amongst the children of my saied Sister Equallie to be Devided Amongst them But if my said Daughter Judith be lyving att thend of the saied three yeares or anye yssue of her bodye then my will ys & soe I Devise & bequeath the saied Hundred & ffiftie pounds to be sett out ^by my executors & overseers^ for the best benefitt of her & her issue & ^the Stock to be^ not ^paied^ vnto her soe long as She shalbe marryed & covert Baron ~~by my executo^{rs} & overseers~~ but my will ys that she shall have the consideracõn yearelie paied vnto her during her lief & after her deceas the saied stock and consideracõn to bee paied to her children if she have Anie & if not to her executo^{rs} or assigns she lyving the saied terme after my deceas Provided that if such husbond as she shall att thend of the saied three yeares be marryed vnto or attaine after doe sufficientle Assure vnto her & thissue of her bodie lands Awnswereable to the porcõn by this my will gyven vnto her & to be adiudged soe by my executo^{rs} & overseers then my will ys that the saied C l^{li} shalbe paied to such husbond as shall make such assurance to his owne vse Itm̃ I gyve & bequeath vnto my saied sister Ione xx^{li} & all my wearing Apparrell to be paied & delivded wthin one yeare after my Deceas And I Doe will & devise vnto her ^the house^ wth thapṗtennc̃s in Stratford wherein she dwelleth for her naturall lief vnder the yearlie Rent of xii^d Itm̃ I gyve & bequeath

vnto her three sonns Willm̄ Harte　　　　　Hart & Michaell Harte
ffyve pounds A peece to be payed w^{th}in one yeare after my deceas
~~to be sett out for her w^{th}in one yeare after my deceas by my executo^{rs}~~
~~wth thadvise & direccōns of my overseers for her best pffitt vntill her~~
~~marriage & then the same wth the increase thereof to be paied vnto~~
　　　　　　　　　　　　　　the saied Elizabeth Hall　(except my brod silver & gilt bole)
her Itm̄ I gyve & bequeath vnto ~~her~~ All my Plate ₐ that I now
have att the date of this my will Itm̄ I gyve & bequeath vnto
the Poore of Stratford aforesaied tenn pounds to Mr. Thomas
Combe my Sword to Thomas Russell Esquier ffyve pounds &
to ffrauncis Collins of the Borough of warr in the countie of warr
gent thirteene pounds Sixe shillings and Eight pence to be paied w^{th}in
　　　　　　　　　　　　　　　　　　　　　　　　　Hamlett Sadler
one Yeare after my deceas Itm̄ I gyve & bequeath to ~~Mr. Richard~~
　　　　　　　　　　to Willm̄ Raynolds gent xxvj^s viij^d to buy him A Ringe
~~Tyler theld~~^r xxvj^s viij^d to buy him A Ringe ₐ to my godson Willm̄
Walker xx^s in gold to Anthonye Nashe gent xxvj^s viii^d & to Mr.
　　　　& to my ffellowes John Hemyngs Richard Burbage & Henry Cundell xxvj^s viij^d Apeece to buy them Ringes
John Nashe xxvj^s viij^d ~~in gold~~ ₐ Itm̄ I Gyve will bequeath & devise vnto
　　　　　　for better enabling of her to pforme this my will & towards the pformans thereof
my Daughter Susanna Hall ₐ All that Capitall messuage or tēnte
　　in Stratford aforesaid
wth thapp̄tennēs ₐ called the newe place wherein I nowe Dwell
& twoe Messuags or tēntes wth thapp̄tennēs scitvat lyeing & being
in Henley Streete w^{th}in the borough of Stratford aforesaied And all
my barnes stables Orchards gardens lands tēnts & hereditam^{ts} whatsoev̄
scituat lyeing & being or to be had Receyved pceyved or taken
w^{th}in the towns Hamletts Villags ffields & grounds of Stratford
vpon Avon Oldstratford Bushopton & Welcombe or in anie of them
in the saied countie of warr And alsoe All that Messuage or
tēnte wth thapp̄tennēs wherein One John Robinson dwelleth scituat
lyeing & being in the blackfriers in London nere the Wardrobe & all
oth^r my lands tēnts & hereditam^{ts} whatsoev To have & to hold All &
singler the saied pmiſſs wth their App^rtennēs vnto the saied Susanna
Hall for & during the terme of her naturall lief & after her
deceas to the first sonne of her bodie lawfullie yssueing & to the
heires Males of the bodie of the saied first Sonne lawfullie
yssueinge & for defalt of such issue to the second Sonne of her
bodie lawfullie issueinge & to the heires Males of the bodie of the
saied Second Sonne lawfullie yfsuinge and for defalt of such
heires to the third Sonne of the bodie of the said Susanna
Lawfullie yssueing & of the heires males of the bodie of the saied third
sonne lawfullie yssueing And for defalt of such yssue the same soe
to be & Remaine to the ffourth ~~Sonne~~ ffyfth Sixte & Seaventh
sonnes of her bodie lawfullie issueing one after Anoth^r & to the heires

Males of the bodies of the saied ffourth fifth Sixte & Seaventh sonnes lawfullie yssueing in such mañn as yt ys before Lymitted to be & Remaine to the first second & third Sonnes of her bodie & to their heires males And for defalt of such issue the saied p̃miſſs to be & Remaine to my sayed Neece Hall & the heires Males of her bodie Lawfullie yssueing & for defalt of such issue to my Daughter Judith & the heires males of her bodie lawfullie issueinge And for defalt of such issue to the Right heires of me the saied Willm̃

Itm I gyve vnto my wief my second best bed wth the furniture
Shackspeare for ever ⸶ Itm̃ I gyve & bequeath to my saied Daughter Judith my broad silver gilt bole All the Rest of my goods Chattels Leases plate Jewels & household stuffe whatsoev̄ after my Detts and Legasies paied & my funerall expences discharged I gyve devise & bequeath to my Sonne in Lawe John Hall gent & my Daughter Susanna his wief whom I ordaine & make executors of this my
                                                                                              the saied
Last will & testamt And I doe intreat & Appoint ⸶ Thomas Russell Esquier & ffrauncis Collins gent to be overseers hereof And doe Revoke All form̃ wills & publishe this to be my last will & testamt In Witness whereof I have herevnto put my hand
~~Seale~~ the Daie & Yeare first above written.

By me William Shakspeare

Witness to the publishing
hereof, Fra: Collyns
Julyus Shawe
John Robinson
Hamnet Sadler
Robert Whattcott

Probatum corā Magr̄i Willim̃i Byrde legum Dcorē Comisson &c. xxiido die menss Junij Anno Dni 1616 Juramto Johannis Hall vnius ex &c. Cui &c. De bene &c. Jurat.—Resv̄at p̃tate &c. Susanne Hall alt ex &c. cu͡ venit &c. petitur.

(Invt ext)